# DO IT YOURSELF

# Growing Plants

## *Plant Life Processes*

Anna Claybourne

Heinemann Library
Chicago, Illinois

Editorial: Louise Galpine and Kate deVilliers
Design: Richard Parker and Tinstar Design Ltd
Illustrations: Oxford designers & illustrators
Picture Research: Mica Brancic and Elaine Willis
Production: Victoria Fitzgerald

Originated by Chroma Graphics (Overseas) Pte. Ltd
Printed and bound in China by Leo Paper Group

12 11 10 09 08
10 9 8 7 6 5 4 3 2 1

**Library of Congress Cataloging-in-Publication Data**
Claybourne, Anna.
Growing plants : plant life processes / Anna Claybourne.
p. cm. -- (Do it yourself science)
Includes bibliographical references and index.
ISBN 978-1-4329-1084-6 (hc) -- ISBN 978-1-4329-1100-3 (pb) 1. Growth (Plants)--Juvenile literature. 2. Plants--Development--Juvenile literature. 3. Growth (Plants)--Experiments--Juvenile literature. 4. Plants--Development--Experiments--Juvenile literature. I. Title.
QK731.C56 2008
580.78--dc22
                                      2007050660

**Acknowledgments**
The publishers would like to thank the following for permission to reproduce photographs: ©Alamy p. **7** (Slim Plantagenate); ©Corbis pp. **4** (The Gallery Collection), **5** (Galen Rowell), **11** (photocuisine/Turiot/Roulier), **23** (Sygma/Collart Herve), **25** (Tania Midgley), **27** (dpa/Andreas Lander), **33** (photocuisine/Poisson d'Avril), **34** (Terry W. Eggers), **39** (Michael Boys), **42** (Ariel Skelley); ©DK Images p. **43** (Peter Anderson); ©FLPA pp. **9**, **20** (Nigel Cattline), **19** (Bob Gibbons), **21** (Holt/Primrose Peacock) **38** (Richard Becker); ©Getty Images pp. **12** (Stone/Cathlyn Melloan), **15** (Stone/Alexander Waiter), **29** (Visuals Unlimited/David Cavagnaro); ©Jupiter Images p. **13** (Botanica/Sang An); ©Rex Features pp. **17** (Robert Harding/Richard Ashworth), **26** (Phil Yeomans), **30** (Shout), **41** (Richard Austin), **37**; ©Science Photo Library p. **35** (Eurelios/Massimo Brega).

Cover photograph of dew drops on a lupin leaf, reproduced with permission of © Getty Images/ Stone/ Rosemary Calvert.

Every effort has been made to contact copyright holders of any material reproduced in this book. Any omissions will be rectified in subsequent printings if notice is given to the publishers.

# Contents

**Warning:** Always wash your hands after touching plants.

Any words appearing in the text in bold, **like this**, are explained in the glossary.

# What Is a Plant?

A plant is a type of living thing. Unlike animals, plants do not move around much. They do not have mouths or eat food in the way that animals do. Instead most plants have **roots** that hold them in place in the soil. The roots take up water and chemicals from the ground. Plants also have green leaves that absorb sunlight and take in gases from the air. With these things, plants have all they need to live and grow.

This ancient Egyptian picture shows people collecting plants they had grown to use as food.

## Growing plants

Plants have existed for millions of years. They were here long before humans, and they do not need us. However, we can help plants grow by taking care of them and protecting them from dangers, such as frost and insects.

## Why grow plants?

You can grow **flowers** in pots to decorate your home or grow a wildlife garden that birds and butterflies will love to visit. Some plants can give you food to eat. Having plants around is good for us, because they make the air healthy for us to breathe. This book explains how plants work and shows you how to grow them.

## Humans and plants

Humans have been helping plants grow for thousands of years. Caring for plants and controlling the way they grow is called **cultivation**. People probably began cultivating plants more than 10,000 years ago, to grow foods such as nuts, wheat, and **fruits**.

All our food basically comes from, or relies, on plants. Fruits, vegetables, **seeds**, beans, and flour are parts of plants. Meat, fish, milk, and eggs come from animals that feed on plants. We get many other things from plants, too, such as wood, bamboo, cotton, and fuel oil.

The giant sequoia is one of the biggest types of living thing on Earth.

### Plants of all sizes

Plants come in many shapes and sizes, from tiny mosses to towering **trees**. The biggest plant around in the world today is the giant sequoia tree. A large giant sequoia can stand more than 260 feet (80 meters) high.

# What Do Plants Need?

## Steps to follow

### Discovering what plants need

For this experiment you will need:

* A handful of dried kidney beans
* Paper towels
* Two clean, empty glass jars
* A dark box or cupboard big enough to fit one of the jars in

**1** Fold a sheet of paper towel in half and fit it around the inside of one jar. Pour some water in until the jar is about a quarter full. Make sure the water is covering the bottom edge of the paper towel.

**2** Push a few beans down the side of the jar, between the glass and the paper (but not into the water).

**3** Do exactly the same with the other jar. Then place one jar on a bright windowsill and the other inside a dark box or cupboard. Check the jars each day and keep the water topped up to the same level.

## What happens?

Over a week or two, the beans in this experiment should **germinate**. This means they open up and start to grow a tiny **root** and a tiny **shoot**. After germinating, a shoot starts to grow leaves. It collects light to help the plant grow.

You may find that the beans in both jars start to germinate. But the plant in the dark does not grow as well as the plant in the light. Plants need light to continue growing.

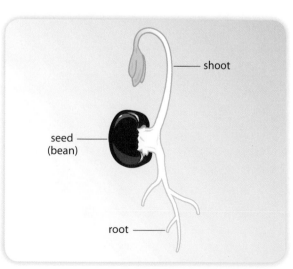

shoot

seed (bean)

root

## Seeds start the job

A bean is a type of **seed**. Seeds are parts of plants that can grow into new plants. A seed contains chemicals that give it the **energy** it needs to germinate. But the energy in the seed runs out, and the plant uses light to continue growing.

The leaves on the **trees** in this forest are all reaching up to fill every gap and collect as much sunlight as they can.

## Photosynthesis

Plants use light, water, and **carbon dioxide** from the air to make food chemicals. Food chemicals are used to build new leaves, seeds, and other parts. This process is called **photosynthesis**, and it happens in the leaves of a plant. The plant gives out spare water and a gas called **oxygen** as waste.

### Gas swap

In addition to providing food, plants help us breathe! Humans, and other animals, breathe in oxygen and breathe out carbon dioxide. Plants take in carbon dioxide and give out oxygen. This means that having plants around helps to replace the oxygen we use up.

# Understanding plants

To take care of a plant and help it grow, you need to remember what it needs.

## Light

Plants need plenty of light. Without enough light, the leaves of a plant turn pale and thin, and it dies.

## Soil

Seeds can germinate without soil. But once they start growing bigger, most plants need to be rooted in the soil. Their roots spread out to take up water. Soil also contains tiny **bacteria** and **minerals** that can help plants grow.

## Water

You water a plant by pouring water into the soil it is standing in. If the soil dries out, the plant will not be able to get water from it. The plant's leaves will wither and droop.

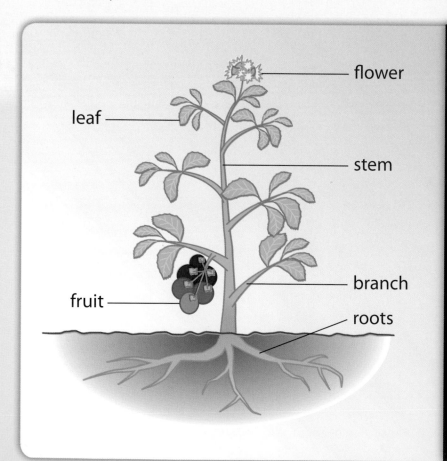

flower

leaf

stem

branch

fruit

roots

A typical flowering plant has these main parts:

- The roots take up water from the soil.

- The **stem** carries water up to the rest of the plant.

- The branches support the leaves.

- The leaves collect sunlight and turn it into food, using photosynthesis.

- The **flowers** contain the parts that allow plants to make seeds.

- The **fruits** contain seeds. A plant's seeds can grow into new plants of the same type, or **species**.

## Plant-care equipment

This basic gardening gear is all you need to grow most plants:

- A watering can
- Plant pots
- Potting **compost**
- Garden trowel (shovel) and garden fork
- Gardening gloves

Gardening tools will last longer if they are kept clean and dry when you are not using them.

## More plant care

There are some more things you can do to help plants grow. Plants' leaves work best if they are clean. If they get dusty, wipe the leaves with tissue paper or wash them under a cold shower. Watch out for plant-eating pests such as snails, slugs, and **aphids**. If you see them, pick them off or brush them away.

## Safety with plants

Some plants can be poisonous, so keep houseplants where small children and pets cannot reach them. Be careful not to put heavy plant pots where they could fall on someone. Keep gardening tools in a safe place where they cannot hurt anyone. Always wash your hands after gardening, in case you have touched any plant poisons or harmful **germs**.

# Plants Indoors

## Steps to follow

**Grow a houseplant from a seed**

You will need:
* An avocado pit
* A small glass jar or cup
* Wooden toothpicks
* A medium-sized plant pot
* Potting **compost**

**1** Fill the jar with water, put the avocado pit in, and leave it to soak overnight.

**2** Take the pit out of the water and carefully insert three toothpicks into it. (You may need an adult to help you.) The sticks should stick out around the pit. With the pointed end of the pit upward, balance the pit on top of the jar and fill the jar with water until about 1 inch (2 cm) of the pit is in water. Stand the jar in a well-lit place and keep the water topped up.

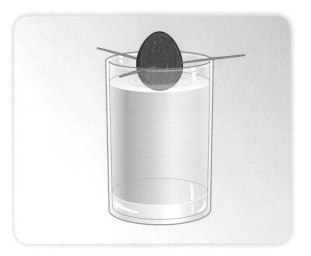

**3** Over several weeks, the pit should **germinate** and grow **roots** and a **shoot**. When you have a pit with roots and a shoot, you can plant it in soil. Fill your plant pot with compost and make a hole in the middle. Gently place the avocado plant in the hole, with the top of the pit and shoot sticking out. Fill in around it with compost and water it well.

## Sending seeds away

Plants cannot move. But they do not want new **seeds** to grow too close to them or they would get crowded out. Instead they need a way to **disperse** (spread out) their seeds. This is where **fruits** come in.

## More seeds to grow

Red pepper seeds grow well if you plant them in soil in a pot. If you live somewhere warm, you can plant a peach pit or a garlic clove right into the soil outdoors.

It is easy to find seeds in many of the fruits we eat, such as apples, oranges, cucumbers, squash, and kiwi fruit.

Fruits attract hungry animals such as birds, squirrels, and humans. When an animal takes a fruit from a **tree**, it may carry it away and drop the seed somewhere else. Birds swallow fruits such as berries, and the seeds come out in their droppings. In this way, plants can send their seeds off to grow far away from themselves, where there is more space.

## A house full of plants

Keeping plants indoors is a great way to begin experimenting with growing plants. It is easier to keep your plants safe from freezing weather and insect pests. Having plants inside your home or classroom is good for you, too. In addition to looking good, plants add **oxygen** to the air, which is great for humans.

## The right light

Plants do best if you place them near a window. Even then, the light will only come from one side. Plants grow toward the light, so you may find that your plants start to lean over toward the window. To fix this, turn your plants around every few days to let them grow the other way and keep their shape.

This plant has leaned over to one side to gather as much light as possible from the window.

## Heading for the light

Plants are **phototropic**, which means they grow toward light. If you put a plant in a tall box and make pieces of cardboard block the way to the top of the box, the plant will bend and twist around the obstacles as it grows toward the light.

## Plant sunburn

If the sun shines through a window and right on to a plant's leaves, it can make them too hot or even burn them. This is especially likely if the windows are made of patterned, shaped glass, like the glass in some bathroom windows. Curves in the glass act like a magnifying glass, making the heat of the sun collect on one point. Plants often grow better beside windows that do not get direct sunlight.

## Pots and containers

Unlike outdoors, where there is soil on the ground, plants indoors have to stand in soil in a pot. The soil in a pot can dry out very easily, so do not forget to water it. You should stand each pot on a plate to catch any water that runs through.

Sometimes houseplants get forgotten about. They can end up hot, dry, dusty, and unwell. You can use a clean paintbrush to clean dust off houseplant leaves.

## Taking a cutting

You will need:

* A plant to take a cutting from. A geranium (a type of small flowering plant, also known as a pelargonium) is perfect.
* Scissors or **pruning shears**
* Potting compost
* A small plant pot
* A watering can

**1** To take the cutting, cut off a branch from the geranium plant. Choose a branch that has two or three pairs of leaves on it, but no **flowers**. Cut it off just below a **leaf joint** (where the leaves branch off).

**2** Carefully pull off the lowest pair of leaves to give the cutting a long stalk. Fill the plant pot with compost, but make sure it is light and crumbly, not packed down hard.

**3** Push the **stem** of the cutting into the compost until it can stand upright on its own. Water well and stand the pot by a window, but not in direct sunlight. The cutting should grow roots and start to grow by itself in a few days. If it doesn't, start again!

## New plants without seeds

This activity shows that you can grow a new plant without a seed. As long as it has leaves, the small cutting works just like a whole plant. Its leaves provide it with food made from sunlight. This means it can grow new roots and other parts and become a separate living thing.

Rubber plants are popular houseplants that grow well from cuttings.

## Which is which?

The plant that gardeners commonly call a geranium is actually called a pelargonium by scientists. It can get confused with another type of geranium, a smaller plant also known as a cranesbill. Pelargoniums such as the one shown on page 14 grow large, colorful flowers.

## Plant clones

Did you know that when you take a cutting, you are **cloning** a plant? Normally, **cells** from two separate plants have to join together to make a seed. This means that, like people, most plants have two "parents" and are a mixture of them both. However, a cutting has only one parent—the plant it came from. It is an exact copy of its parent, or a "clone." Most plants can be cloned quite easily using cuttings.

## Steps to follow

**1** Lie your bottle on its side. Use the spoon to put the gravel inside it and spread it out. Then add a layer of compost about 2 inches (5 cm) deep.

**2** Using the spoon, scoop out a hole in the compost for each plant. Then remove the plants from their pots, lift them into the bottle, and set them in the holes. Use the fork to fill in around each plant with compost and pat it down.

**3** Water the bottle garden using a watering can with a long spout. If you don't have one, carefully pour water into the neck of the bottle using a jug.

**Warning**: Large bottles can be heavy. You may need to get help to lift your bottle garden on to a table or windowsill.

# Grow a bottle garden

You will need:

* A clear glass jar or bottle with a wide neck
* A handful of gravel
* Potting compost
* A kitchen fork and a spoon
* A watering can with a long spout
* Three or four very small potted plants ready for planting, available from a garden center. Look for dwarf or miniature **varieties** of plants such as ferns, **herbs**, and flowering plants.

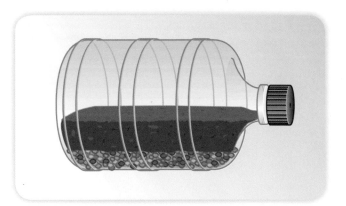

## Mini garden tools

Full-sized garden gear is too big for a bottle garden, so you will need to borrow a spoon and fork from the kitchen. (Make sure they are washed well afterward.) If they are not long enough, use sticky tape or a rubber band to fix their handles to something longer such as chopsticks or wooden spoon handles.

## World in a bottle

A bottle garden is like a whole miniature garden that you can keep indoors! Bottle gardens do not need to be watered as much as other houseplants. The water **evaporates** from the soil and the plants into the air in the bottle. It collects on the sides of the bottle and eventually runs back down into the soil. The bottle lets in light but holds heat inside, keeping the plants warm.

This huge **greenhouse** works in the same way as your bottle garden— by trapping heat and **moisture** inside.

# Plants Outdoors

## Steps to follow

**Warning**: You will need an adult to help you hang the basket up. It must be hung on a hook or nail that is firmly fixed into an outdoor wall, overhead beam, or archway where sun and rain can reach it.

## Hanging herb garden

You will need:

* A hanging basket
* Potting **compost**
* Four or five small **herb** plants, such as oregano, rosemary, mint, basil, or thyme
* A trowel (shovel)
* A watering can

1. Almost fill the basket with compost, and pat it down gently. Meanwhile, water the plants in their pots and leave them to stand.

2. Use a trowel or your hand to make a hole in the compost for each plant. Evenly space them around the basket.

3. Remove the plants from their pots and press each one into its hole in the compost. Press down the compost around them. Water the basket well.

## What are herbs?

Herbs are small, leafy plants with strong scents and flavors. Humans have been using them for thousands of years to flavor food. Many herbs can also be used as medicines. If you are using herbs in food, pull the leaves off the stalks and wash the herbs carefully before eating them. Ask an adult to help you chop herbs with a knife or scissors. Here are some things you can do with herbs:

| Herb | Recipe |
|------|--------|
| Mint | Float the leaves in lemonade or chop and add them to boiled potatoes or peas. |
| Oregano | Chop it finely and sprinkle on to pizza or stir it into pasta sauce. |
| Rosemary | Chop it finely and sprinkle it on to lamb or butternut squash before cooking. |
| Basil | Eat the fresh, washed leaves in a salad with tomatoes and mozzarella cheese. |
| Thyme | Stir chopped leaves into stews and soups. |

## A place in the sun

Outdoors is the natural place for most plants to be. They get lots of natural sunlight and are watered by the rain. They can stretch out their **roots** to reach for water deep in the earth. Natural **bacteria** found in the soil can be good for plants, and worms under the ground tunnel through the soil, making it light and airy.

## Outdoor dangers

Outdoor life can also create problems for plants. Some die if the weather gets too cold and frosty. Wind, hail, and heavy rain can damage delicate **stems**, leaves, and **flowers**. Pests such as slugs, snails, and caterpillars love to find plants and eat them.

This cabbage plant is being nibbled by caterpillars.

## Short or long life?

**Annuals** are plants that live for one season. You plant them in the spring, and they live through the summer, then die when winter comes. They leave behind **seeds** that can grow the following year. They include many types of small garden flowers, such as cosmos and petunias.

**Perennials**, such as black-eyed Susans, are tougher plants that can live in the garden for many years. They may die down in the winter, but their roots are still there and grow up again in spring.

You can also grow **shrubs** and **trees** in a garden. These plants have tough, woody stems or trunks and grow all year round.

## Soil sorting

Did you know there are different types of soil?

**Clay soil** is thick, heavy, and sticky when wet. It is hard to dig and can get waterlogged. Adding some sand makes clay soil better for plants.

**Sandy soil** has a light, sandy, gritty feel. Water **drains** through it easily, so plants can dry out. Adding lots of compost makes sandy soil better for plants.

**Loam** is soil with a mixture of sand and clay and is the best for growing plants.

This buddleia is a flowering shrub that can grow as big as a small tree. Its flowers have a sweet smell and attract butterflies.

## Plant a tree

You will need:

* A small potted tree from a garden center. An apple, pear, or cherry tree is perfect.
* A garden fork and spade
* Compost
* A watering can
* An adult to help you

**1** Decide where you want to plant your tree. It should not be too close to other plants, and there should be plenty of sunlight and not too much wind. Using the fork, turn the soil over in an area about 6 feet (2 m) across, around where you plan to plant the tree. This means digging into the soil, lifting it up, and breaking it apart to loosen it.

**2** Water the tree well while it is standing in its pot and leave it to soak in. Using the spade, dig a hole in the middle of the area you have prepared. The hole should be about 12 inches (30 cm) deep and about 3 feet (1 m) across.

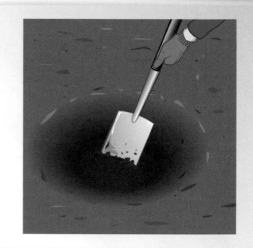

**3** Lie the tree on its side and carefully remove its pot. Use your hands to gently loosen the tree's roots and spread them out. Now stand the tree in the hole, making sure the base of the trunk is just above ground level. One person should hold the tree steady while another fills the hole in with a mixture of soil and compost. Pack the soil and compost down firmly around the tree and water it well.

## What is a tree?

A tree is a type of big, tough plant. Because trees are large, they have to be strong enough to hold up their own weight. Their stems (trunks) grow thick and tough, forming a substance we call wood. Trees take years to reach their full size, and they live longer than most other plants.

## Did you know?

The oldest known tree in the world is growing in California. It is a bristlecone pine and is thought to be more than 4,000 years old!

The Amazon rainforest in Brazil contains billions of trees. It is shrinking every day because the trees are being cut down for wood and to make space for farmland.

# Flowers

## Steps to follow

**Funky fuchsias**

You will need:

* A cutting from a fuchsia plant, or a small fuchsia plant from a garden center
* Potting **compost**
* A plant pot
* A hanging basket or other container
* A clear plastic bag, such as a food storage bag
* A trowel (shovel) and scissors
* A glass of water
* A watering can

**1** To take a cutting from a fuchsia, use scissors to cut off a stalk just below a **leaf joint**, leaving three pairs of leaves on the stalk. Pull off the lowest pair of leaves to leave a long bare stalk. Stand the cutting in a glass of water.

**2** Fill a plant pot with compost and push the cutting into the compost. Water the cutting well. If you put a clear plastic bag loosely over the cutting for a few days, it will keep water and warmth inside, helping the plant to grow.

**3** When your fuchsia has grown bigger and stronger—or if you buy a fuchsia plant from a garden center—it can be planted indoors or outdoors. Fuchsias make good houseplants, but they can also grow in hanging baskets, in outdoor containers, or in the ground.

## Fuchsia flowers

When your fuchsia grows **flowers**, you will see that they are made up of several parts. The **petals** form a round cup shape that usually hangs downward. Out of this hang long stalk-like shapes, called the **stigma** and **stamens**.

A large fuchsia plant can have hundreds of flowers and look very colorful.

## Plant varieties

When you go to a garden center, you will see that fuchsias—and many other plants—come in different **varieties**. There are more than 7,000 varieties of fuchsia! Different varieties have different colors, shapes, and sizes. Gardeners create different varieties by choosing plants for particular qualities and breeding them.

## Plant collectors

In the 1700s and 1800s, many **botanists** (plant scientists) went exploring and collected all kinds of plants from around the world. They took wild plant **seeds** home and **cultivated** them to create garden plants for everyone to use. Fuchsias, for example, come from South America and New Zealand—but now they are grown all over the world.

## What are flowers for?

We think of flowers as the pretty part of a plant. We use them as decoration and for their scents. But for a plant, flowers have a far more important job to do. They allow a plant to make seeds, so that it can **reproduce** and make new plants.

## Inside a flower

All flowers have the same basic parts. The petals surround the flower and give it color. Inside the petals are stalks called stamens. They hold up the **anthers**, which release a dusty yellow substance made up of tiny **pollen cells**. In the middle is another stalk called the stigma. It collects pollen from other flowers. At the base of the stigma is the **ovary**, where seeds are made.

This diagram shows a flower cut in half, so you can see all the parts inside clearly.

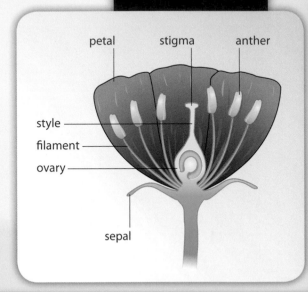

petal · stigma · anther · style · filament · ovary · sepal

This field of flowers is being grown in the Netherlands for the cut flower industry.

## Making a seed

To make a seed, pollen from one flower has to land on the stigma of another flower. The pollen sends a tube down through the stigma to the ovary. A pollen cell joins with a cell inside the ovary to make a seed. This is called **pollination**.

You can see some pollen on this bee's head as it leaves a tulip flower. Some of the pollen will brush off on to the next flower the bee visits.

## Invitation to insects

How does pollen get from one flower to another? Sometimes the wind carries pollen through the air. But many plants use a more reliable pollination method—insects. Insects visit flowers to feed on them and get covered in pollen. When they visit another flower, they leave some pollen behind.

To give insects a reason to visit them, flowers contain a sweet liquid called **nectar**. It provides food for butterflies, bees, and many other insects. Plants have large, bright flowers and sweet scents to help insects find them easily.

## Flower factories

Every day, millions of flowers are harvested. We buy them to decorate our homes or to give as gifts. We also grow flowers for their perfume. It takes around 1,500 rose flowers to make just one teaspoonful of pure rose oil!

# Plants as Food

## Steps to follow

**1** You can grow your beans in a large tub or in the ground. The best time to **sow** the seeds is in spring. Use a garden fork to turn over the soil, and add a few handfuls of compost. Then use the three bamboo canes to make a tepee shape about 2 feet (60 cm) across. Tie the tops of the canes together with twine. (Ask an adult to help.)

**2** Plant two seeds at the base of each cane, one on each side. Push the seeds into the soil to 2 inches (5 cm) deep. Water the soil well.

**3** Keep the bean plants well watered as they start to grow. When they are 3 inches (7 cm) tall, pull out one of the two plants at the base of each cane, leaving just one. (Planting two means there is a backup if one fails to grow. If only one has grown, leave it.) The bean plants should wind around the canes and grow up to the top of the tepee.

**Ready to eat**: The beans are ready to pick when they are green and firm. Pick the whole pods with the beans inside. To cook your beans, wash them and then boil or steam the pods for a few minutes (with an adult to help you) and eat them whole.

### Grow your own beanstalk

You will need:

* 6 scarlet runner bean **seeds**
* 3 bamboo garden canes, about 6 feet (2 m) long
* Compost
* Garden twine or string
* A large garden fork
* A watering can

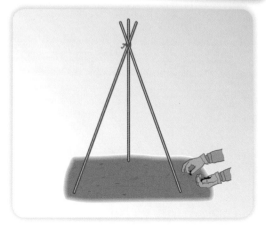

## What are beans?

A bean is a type of seed that grows inside a pod. Beans are members of a plant family called **legumes**, along with peas and lentils. Legumes are a very healthy food. They are also good for the soil. As they grow, they add a chemical called **nitrogen** to the soil, which is good for other plants.

## Jack's beanstalk

In the fairytale *Jack and the Beanstalk*, a magical giant beanstalk grows overnight. Though they do not grow that fast, scarlet runner beans do grow very quickly. They may have inspired the magic beanstalk in the story.

Scarlet runner beans look like this when they are ready to pick.

## Plant food

When you think about eating plants, you might think of something like an apple, salad leaves, or celery stalks. But it is not just **fruits** and vegetables that come from plants. The wheat that makes bread, the corn in cornflakes, and the sugar and cocoa in a bar of chocolate are all plant foods.

Many people pick wild berries every fall to add to pies, cakes, or drinks.

## No meat

Humans have traditionally been **omnivores**, which means we eat both plants and animals. However, some people choose not to eat animals. **Vegetarians** do not eat meat from animals, though they may eat animal products such as eggs, milk, and honey. **Vegans** do not eat anything that comes from animals, including milk, eggs, and cheese. They only eat plant foods.

## The food chain

Plants are the basis of the **food chain**. This is the name for the sequence of living things that feed on other living things. It starts with plants, which make their food using **energy** from the sun. Animals such as insects, rabbits, deer, and sheep eat these plants. These animals in turn give energy to predators such as foxes, birds of prey, and wolves when they are eaten. In some food chains these predators may also be eaten by other, even larger, predators.

If plants did not exist, animals could not exist, either, because there would be nothing for them to eat. We all depend on plants to stay alive.

This picture shows a simple ocean food chain in the Antarctic. Plankton (tiny animal and plant life that float in water) are the basis of this chain.

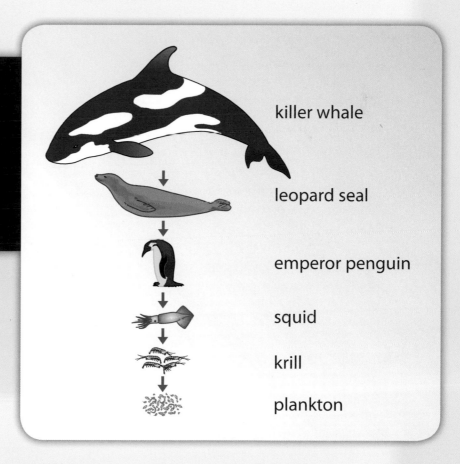

killer whale

leopard seal

emperor penguin

squid

krill

plankton

## Wild food

Thousands of years ago, early humans ate plants that they could find in the wild such as fruits, nuts, and berries. Over time, we learned to farm plants so that we could grow the food plants we wanted, where we wanted them. But you can still find plant food growing wild. For example, blackberries grow on prickly wild bramble bushes and can be collected every fall. (Never pick or eat a wild berry unless you are with an adult and know it is safe to eat.)

## Steps to follow

**1** You can plant strawberries in the spring or fall. Place the pot in a sunny spot, away from strong winds. Fill the pot with compost, and dig and turn it over using the fork. If you are using a strawberry pot, which has several small openings, it may be easier to dig the soil with a kitchen fork. (Wash it well afterward.)

**2** Use your fingers to make a hollow in the compost for each plant. Remove the plants from their pots and place them in the hollows. Make sure only the **roots** are below the soil. Press the compost back around each plant and water them well.

**3** If you are not using a strawberry pot, you can place flat pebbles around the base of each plant to protect it. On top, add a ring of broken eggshells. The pebbles will prevent weeds and hold **moisture** in the soil. The sharp eggshells will stop slugs from reaching the plants. In cold weather, you can also cover the strawberry plants with plastic bags to keep them warm.

## Strawberries for dessert

You will need:

* A large, wide plant pot, or a strawberry pot, that has several openings all over it
* Compost
* A small garden trowel (shovel) and fork
* About five small strawberry plants
* A watering can
* Flat pebbles and washed, broken eggshells

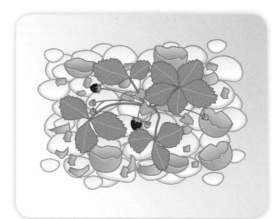

## Manure

Your strawberries will grow even better if you mix **manure** into the compost before you start. Manure is made of the droppings of animals such as horses and cows. Though it does not sound very pleasant, it contains lots of important chemicals and **bacteria** that help plants to grow. You can buy it at garden centers.

## Seeds on the outside

Strawberries are unusual fruits because they have their seeds on the outside and not in the middle. Look closely at a strawberry. You will see seeds dotted all over its surface. A strawberry can have up to 200 seeds.

## What are crops?

Crops are plants that are grown to make products that can be used or sold. Most crops are turned into food. The world's biggest crops include cereal plants such as wheat, rice, and corn. Crops can be grown to make other things, too—for example, cotton plants are made into cloth, and cork **trees** are grown for their cork bark. Around 15 percent of all the world's land is used for growing crops.

This huge combine harvester cuts wheat plants, picks them up, and separates the stalks from the kernels.

## GM crops

**GM crops** stands for "genetically modified crops." In the past 50 years, scientists have learned how to change the **genes** of living things. Genes are the instructions inside **cells** that control the way living things grow and work. GM crops are crops that have had some of their genes changed.

For example, one type of GM strawberry plant has a gene from a deep-sea fish added to it. This gene makes the plant produce a substance that stops it from freezing in frosty weather. Because the GM strawberries survive cold weather, they make better crops. However, some people think that changing the genes of plants is not a good idea.

## Creating crops

Crop plants usually look different from wild plants. Just as gardeners have **cultivated** garden plants, farmers have cultivated crops. One way to do this is by **selective breeding**. Over the centuries, farmers have chosen the best plants from their crops—such as the wheat plant with the biggest, fattest grains, or the strawberry plant with the sweetest, tastiest strawberries. They use seeds from these plants to grow the next crop. Over time, this turns wild plants into more and more useful crop **varieties**.

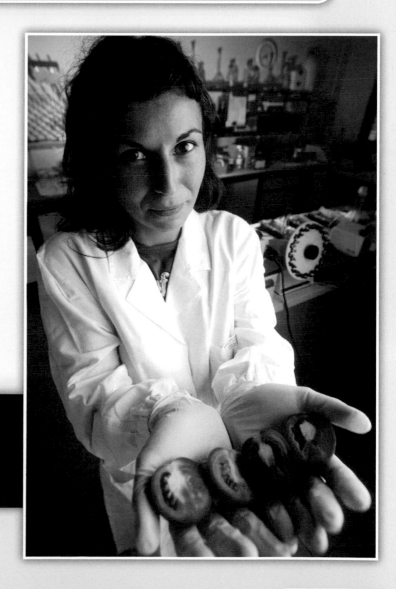

The tomato on the right has been genetically modified to prevent it from growing seeds.

# A Wildlife Garden

## Steps to follow

### Lavender for bees

You will need:

* A medium-sized plant pot
* Compost
* Two handfuls of sand
* A handful of pebbles
* A small trowel (shovel) and fork
* A small lavender plant

**1** Put the pebbles into the bottom of the pot. Fill it almost full with compost, add the sand, and use the trowel to mix the sand and compost.

**2** Dig out a hole in the soil with the trowel. Remove the lavender plant from its pot and plant it in the hole. Press the soil down around it and water well.

**3** Place the pot outdoors in a sunny spot. Now watch out for bees! They will detect the lavender and come to feed on its **flowers**.

## Scents and insects

Flowers have scents to help insects find them—and the tasty **nectar** inside them. When a honeybee visits a flower such as lavender, the flower's scent rubs off on the bee. This may tell the other bees what flowers are nearby.

Not all flowers smell sweet, though. The huge rafflesia flower, which grows in rainforests in Southeast Asia, smells of stinking rotten meat! The smell attracts flies, because they often lay their eggs in rotting meat. They visit the flower and help to **pollinate** it.

## Useful lavender

Besides attracting bees, lavender will make your garden smell good. Its scent is said to have a calming effect, so people sometimes use pillows filled with dried lavender to help them sleep. It has also been used as a medicine for thousands of years. The ancient Greeks and Romans used its oil to help heal wounds.

On this lavender farm in France, the lavender is grown in long rows of dome-shaped bushes.

## Blues for bees

Bees especially like blue and purple flowers. Their eyesight is different from human eyesight. They can see ultraviolet (deep purple) light that is invisible to us. Blue and purple flowers give out more of this light, so bees can spot them easily. Other blue flowers that bees love include cornflowers, ceanothus, and love-in-a-mist (also called nigella).

## A home for wildlife

When you garden, it is a good idea to think about helping wildlife. Wild plants and animals need to find places to live. There are three main ways you can help:

- Have lots of different types of plants, to provide food and shelter for different types of wildlife.

- Choose plants that are especially useful to animals—for example, plants with berries for birds or blue flowers for bees.

- Don't be too neat! It is good for your garden to have some wild areas where wild flowers and weeds can grow, and where wild animals can hide and take shelter.

### Keep it green

Try not to use chemical **weedkillers** or **pesticides** (pest killers). These fill your garden with poisonous chemicals that are bad for wildlife. If you want to keep pests away from plants such as strawberries, cover the plants with garden netting instead. You can also encourage natural predators. For example, let nettles grow, as ladybugs like them. In return, the ladybugs will eat your **aphids**.

Not all bees live in hives! This wild bumblebee is going into its nest in a wall.

## Which plants to choose?

Many of the plants mentioned in this book are good for wildlife. Buddleia is also known as the "butterfly bush" because butterflies love it. **Herbs** and **fruit trees** have flowers that provide nectar for bees and butterflies to feed on. Fuchsias have flowers for bees and berries for birds. Birds also like strawberries, though you might not want them to eat all of yours!

## Wildflower corner

Make a "wildflower corner"—leave a corner of your garden wild. Do not cut the grass or pick the weeds. Buy a package of mixed wildflower **seeds** and scatter them around your wild corner.

Lots of different plants, messy areas, bushes, and **shrubs** give wildlife a place to hide.

## Animal shelters

Thick bushes, hedges, and thorny plants make safe places for birds to hide and nest. Piles of plant waste, such as fallen leaves and long grass, make good shelters for insects, spiders, and wild mice.

## Grow sunflowers

You will need:

* Several sunflower seeds. (Use seeds from a garden center. Those sold in supermarkets as food are often cooked and will not grow.)
* A garden fork
* A watering can

## A feast for wildlife

Sunflowers provide nectar for bees, butterflies, and even hummingbirds. Other birds will also visit to eat the sunflower seeds.

**1** Sunflower seeds should be planted outside in spring, after any frosty weather is over. They need a very sunny place to grow. First, use the fork to dig and turn over the soil. Then, plant the seeds in a row, spaced about 12 inches (30 cm) apart. Push each seed about 1 inch (2 cm) down into the soil.

**2** Water the sunflowers often. As the plants start to grow, pull out any weeds that grow around them, to give them plenty of space. It will take about 10 to 12 weeks for the sunflowers to grow to their full height and grow flowers.

## Many flowers in one

If you look closely at a sunflower, you will see it does not look quite like a normal flower. It has bright yellow **petals** around the outside and a large, disc-shaped area of darker parts in the middle. In fact, a sunflower is not a single flower. It is a **composite flower**, made up of hundreds of smaller flowers (**florets**) joined together.

Your sunflowers will probably grow taller than you—and maybe taller than the tallest person you know!

## Follow the sun

When your sunflowers have formed flower buds, watch them carefully. Are they moving? Sunflower buds are **heliotropic**. That means they turn to face the sun as it moves across the sky each day. Once a sunflower opens its petals, it stops moving.

## Sunflower race

You could have a sunflower race. Label each person's sunflower with his or her name by writing it on a wooden lollipop stick and sticking it in the ground nearby. Measure the sunflowers every week and see whose grows fastest and tallest. Sunflowers often reach heights of 6 to 10 feet (2 to 3 m). Some have been known to grow as tall as 26 feet (8 m)—that is as high as a house!

# Growing and Gardening

Growing plants is a great hobby. Anyone can do it—whether you have a garden at home, a school garden, a patio, or just a pot on a windowsill. As you grow plants, you will learn more and more about them. You will also be able to make your home or garden more beautiful—and you will see more birds and butterflies, too. Gardening even helps you stay fit and healthy. It is something you can do together with your friends or family, and it does not have to cost much money!

Growing your own food, harvesting it, and eating it makes a fun, useful, and money-saving hobby.

Here are a few more plants you might like to try growing:

- Daffodils grow from a type of **root** called a **bulb**. You plant the bulbs in the fall to grow and blossom in the spring.
- Poppies are pretty **flowers** that grow from tiny black **seeds**.
- Tomatoes are fast-growing plants. You plant the seeds in late spring in pots or hanging baskets. With lots of water and sunshine, they will give you dozens of tasty tomatoes.

Rainwater is stored deep underground. We need to keep as much land as we can green and uncovered, so that the rain can soak in.

## A greener world

As you know, plants are not just for fun. In fact, you could say they are the most important things on our planet! By growing plants, you can change the world and help the planet. Here's how:

- Plants provide food and homes for wildlife—so growing plants helps more living things to survive.

- Land that is kept as a garden is better for the planet than land that is paved or covered with concrete. The plants give out **oxygen** into the air. Rainwater will soak into the soil, instead of flowing away over the surface. This helps to keep water supplies stocked up because water is often collected from underground.

- If you grow your own **fruits** and vegetables, you will save **energy**. Those foods will grow right next to you instead of having to be transported long distances, stocked in a store, and cooled in a refrigerator.

# Glossary

**annual** plant that grows, makes seeds, and dies within a year

**anther** part of a flower that produces pollen. The pollen helps plants make new seeds.

**aphid** type of tiny insect that feeds on plants

**bacteria** tiny living things found in soil, water, and inside other living things. Some bacteria can cause diseases.

**botanist** scientist who studies plants

**bulb** type of underground root that can grow into a new plant

**carbon dioxide** gas found in the air that plants need. They use it along with sunlight to make food.

**cell** tiny unit that makes up living things. A typical plant is made of billions of cells.

**clay soil** type of thick, smooth, heavy soil

**clone** make an exact copy of a living thing, such as a plant

**composite flower** flower made up of many smaller flowers joined together. Sunflowers are composite flowers.

**compost** rich soil-like substance made from rotted plants

**cultivation** taking care of plants, breeding them, and helping them to grow

**disperse** spread out over a wide area

**drain** flow away easily. Water drains well through sandy soil.

**energy** power to grow or do work. Plants need energy to grow new leaves and other parts.

**evaporate** change from a liquid into a gas. Water evaporates quickly in strong sunshine.

**floret** one of the small flowers that make up a composite flower

**flower** part of a plant that makes pollen and seeds. Flowers are often brightly colored.

**food chain** way that living things are linked by their food. An example of a simple food chain is: pondweed is eaten by tadpoles, which are eaten by a newt.

**fruit** part of a plant that surrounds a seed. Many fruits are sweet and make a tasty food.

**gene** instruction found inside cells. Genes control the way living things grow and work.

**germ** tiny living thing that can cause diseases. Some types of bacteria are germs.

**germinate** begin to grow from a seed into a plant. As a seed germinates, it grows a root and a shoot.

**GM crops** (short for "genetically modified crops") plants that have had their genes changed. This is usually done to make them into more useful crops.

**greenhouse** enclosed structure used to grow plants. Botanic gardens often have greenhouses where tropical plants are grown.

**heliotropic** having the ability to turn toward the sun

**herb** small, leafy plant with a strong flavor or scent. Herbs are often used in cooking or medicine.

**leaf joint** place where a plant's leaves join a stem. When taking a cutting, you cut just below a leaf joint.

**legume** plant that has seeds growing inside pods. Peas and beans are legumes.

**loam** type of soil made from a mixture of sandy soil and clay soil

**manure** animal droppings

**mineral** non-living natural substance. Rocks and metals are minerals.

**moisture** dampness or wetness

**nectar** sweet liquid made by flowers. Some types of insects and other animals feed on it.

**nitrogen** gas found in the air and in soil. Nitrogen helps plants to grow.

**omnivore** living thing that eats both plants and animals. Chimpanzees are omnivores.

**ovary** part of a flower where seeds are made. The ovary sometimes swells to form a fruit around the seed.

**oxygen** gas found in the air. Humans and other animals need to breathe in oxygen.

**perennial** plant that can live through more than one year

**pesticide** chemical used to kill garden pests such as aphids. Pesticides can be poisonous to other animals, too.

**petal** colored part surrounding a flower. Petals help to attract insects.

**photosynthesis** process plants use to turn sunlight and carbon dioxide into food

**phototropic** ability to reach or grow toward the light. Plants are phototropic.

**pollen** yellow substance made by flowers. Pollen helps plants to make seeds.

**pollination** process of pollen moving from one flower to another. This allows it to form seeds.

**pruning shears** garden tool used for cutting plants

**reproduce** make more living things of the same species

**root** part of a plant that reaches down into the soil. Roots take in water for the plant to use.

**sandy soil** type of soil that contains a lot of sand

**seed** part of a plant that can grow into a new plant of the same species

**selective breeding** choosing the most useful plants for breeding. This helps us to develop useful crops.

**shoot** first stem that grows out of a seed when it begins to germinate. The shoot later grows leaves.

**shrub** tough, woody plant

**sow** plant seeds

**species** particular type of living thing

**stamen** part of a flower that holds up the anther

**stem** main stalk of a plant. It connects the leaves to the roots.

**stigma** part of a flower that collects pollen from other flowers

**tree** large plant with a thick, tough stalk called a trunk. The trunk is made of wood.

**variety** different color, shape, and style of the same basic type of plant. There are many varieties of roses.

**vegan** someone who eats only plant food. Vegans eat no animal products at all.

**vegetarian** someone who does not eat meat. However, vegetarians do eat animal products such as cheese.

**weedkiller** chemical used to kill weeds (unwanted plants). Weedkillers can also kill healthy plants.

# Find Out More

## Books

Burnie, David. *Eyewitness: Plant*. New York: Dorling Kindersley, 2004.

A detailed exploration of the world of plants, with lots of amazing photos.

Johnson, Sue, and Cheryl Evans. *Starting Gardening*. Tulsa, Okla.: Usborne/EDC, 2003.

An easy introduction to gardening skills.

Spohn, Rebecca. *Ready, Set, Grow! A Kid's Guide to Gardening*. Tucson, Ariz.: Good Year, 2007.

A fun guide to gardening, with lots of things to try.

Whitehouse, Patricia. *Plants: Science Fair Projects*. Chicago: Heinemannn Library, 2008.

Science projects with a plant theme that are useful for schoolwork.

## Websites

Plant Basics at Biology4Kids

**www.biology4kids.com/files/plants_main.html**

Facts about plants, along with pictures and quizzes.

Plant Experiments for Kids

**www.mgonline.com/experimentsforkids.html**

Five fascinating plant experiments to try.

Plants for Kids

**www.plantsforkids.com**

Information on all types of interesting plants.

# Botanical gardens to visit

A botanical garden is like a zoo for plants. It is a park or large garden where amazing plants from around the world are grown and studied. There are many botanical gardens around the world, and most are open to the public. Many also have interesting websites.

## United States

### Desert Botanical Garden
1201 N. Galvin Parkway
Phoenix, Arizona 85008
www.dbg.org

### New York Botanical Garden
Bronx River Parkway at Fordham Road
Bronx, New York 10458
www.nybg.org

### U.S. Botanic Garden
245 First Street, S.W.
Washington, D.C. 20024
www.usbg.gov

### Chicago Botanic Garden
1000 Lake Cook Road
Glencoe, Illinois 60022
www.chicagobotanic.org

### Los Angeles County Arboretum & Botanic Garden
301 North Baldwin Avenue
Arcadia, California 91007
www.arboretum.org

### The State Botanical Garden of Georgia
2450 South Milledge Avenue
Athens, Georgia 30605
www.uga.edu/botgarden

### San Francisco Botanical Garden
9th Avenue at Lincoln Way
San Francisco, California 94122
www.sfbotanicalgarden.org

## Canada

### Royal Botanical Gardens
680 Plains Road West
Burlington ON, L7T 4H4
Canada
www.rbg.ca/index.html

# Index